ART DECO

MAILBOXES

AN ILLUSTRATED
DESIGN HISTORY

ART DECO

MAILBOXES

AN ILLUSTRATED DESIGN HISTORY

Karen Greene & Lynne Lavelle

W. W. NORTON & COMPANY
NEW YORK · LONDON

For information about permission to reproduce selections from this book, write to
Permissions, W. W. Norton & Company, Inc., 500 Fifth Avenue, New York, NY 10110

For information about special discounts for bulk purchases, please contact W. W. Norton
Special Sales at specialsales@wwnorton.com or 800-233-4830

Manufacturing by KHL Printing Co. Pte Ltd
Book design by Chin-Yee Lai
Production manager: Leeann Graham

Library of Congress Cataloging-in-Publication Data

Greene, Karen (Karen J.)
Art deco mailboxes : an illustrated design history / Karen Greene & Lynne Lavelle. —
First Edition.
    pages cm
Includes bibliographical references and index.
ISBN 978-0-393-73340-2 (pbk.)
1. Mailboxes—United States. 2. Mail-chutes. 3. Decoration and ornament, Architec-
tural—United States. 4. Decoration and ornament—United States—Art deco. I. Lavelle,
Lynne. II. Title.
HE6497.M3G74 2014
745.593—dc23
2014015732

W. W. Norton & Company, Inc., 500 Fifth Avenue, New York, N.Y. 10110
www.wwnorton.com
W. W. Norton & Company Ltd., Castle House, 75/76 Wells Street, London W1T 3QT

1 3 5 7 9 0 8 6 4 2

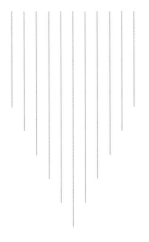

DEDICATION

This book is dedicated with much love to my husband, Jack, and my daughter, Emily. They managed to get along at home without me while I was traveling around the country chasing mailboxes. Thank you for your patience, encouragement, and support, and for allowing me the space to immerse myself in the art and history of the mailbox.

I would also like to dedicate this book to all the building doormen, security guards, supers and building managers whom I encountered on my journeys. They allowed me access to their lobbies, and did not laugh too hard when I explained my mission.

ACKNOWLEDGMENTS

First, I would like to express my profound gratitude to Nancy Green, my editor at W.W. Norton, who loved the idea of this project from the beginning, and who, with her assistant, Ben Yarling, patiently kneaded and shaped it to completion. She also encouraged me to get out of my New York City architectural comfort zone and explore the postal riches of other cities.

I would like to thank the librarians who helped with this project: Caroline Gifford and Vinny Ritgliano of the New York Public Library's Art and Architecture Department, who suggested the 1931 issue of *Architecture* with its portfolio of mailboxes; Nancy Martin of the Rush Rhees Library of the University of Rochester, for access to Cutler production line photos; Erin Schreiner of the Avery Library of Columbia University and Kathryn Murano of the Rochester Science Museum Library, both of whom allowed me access to original Cutler advertising brochures, and who gave permission for their inclusion here; and Robert Scheffel of the Rochester Central Library's Local History and Geneology Division for his assistance with Cutler family and Rochester civic historical materials. Librarians are truly the keepers and protectors of our history and culture. I would also like to thank FTI Consulting, Inc. for the permission to include Cutler materials, and Mr. Peter Sarratori, President of Rochester Lead Works, the firm now on the site of the original Cutler factory. He was a gracious host and took me on a tour of the offices and original factory floor.

I would also like to thank all the residential building co-op boards, hotels, commercial building management companies, and building owners who graciously granted permission for the inclusion of photos of their mailboxes herein, and who had the foresight to preserve these beautiful mailboxes in their lobbies. These include: The Adler Group, ASI Management, Ashforth Management, Blue Woods Management, Beacon Capital Partners, Braun Realty Management, Capitol Management, CBCR Reliant Realty, CBRE, LH Charney, Colliers, George Comfort & Sons, the Common Ground Organization, Cushman Wakefield, the Durst Organization, Douglas Elliman, First Service Residential, the Feil Organization, FREG, Gotham Holdings, SL Green, Izard Realty, JDS Development Group, Kew Management, JEM Realty, JEMB Realty, KTR Management, Lincoln Properties, MPI Realty, Magnum Real Estate Group, Marc Realty, MBRES, Metroloft NYC, the MTA, Newmark Grabb Knight Frank, NYCHHC, PMC Property Group, Realty Trust Corp., Rose Associates, Stonehenge Management, RFR Realty, Silverstein Properties, Sorgente Holdings, SWIG Equities, Tishman Speyer, Vornado Realty Trust, Winthrop Management, and the Witkoff Group.

Finally, I would like to thank Robert Arthur King, photographer and author of *Faces in Stone: Architectural Sculpture in New York City* (Norton, 2008). His work and approach to urban photography reminded me of how important it is to really look at our cities, at the things we pass by every day, and to preserve our architectural heritage.

CONTENTS

ART DECO

MAILBOXES

AN ILLUSTRATED
DESIGN HISTORY

INTRODUCTION

When the Elwood Building opened its doors on the northeast corner of Rochester, New York's State and Main streets in 1879, its architect, James Goold Cutler, saw room for improvement. At a time when one five-cent stamp could deliver a letter to the other side of the world, employees of lawyer Frank W. Elwood had to carry mail from the seventh-story top floor to the lobby by hand, and down the stairs—as everyone else did. Cities were expanding vertically, rather than horizontally, in response to increasing land values and inexpensive mass-produced steel. Buildings were rising in height.

The original Cutler factory on Anderson Avenue, Rochester, NY. From Cutler brochure, 1937.

INTRODUCTION

On September 11, 1883, Cutler received Patent No. 284,951, for an innovative mail-delivery system. His invention, mailbox and chute, comprised a wall-mounted or recessed container at the ground-floor level, fed by a glass-paneled vertical tube that rose the building's height. Mail would be deposited through slots on each floor, where the chute could be also be unlocked in the event that a letter got stuck. The system would, Cutler said, "enable persons upon the different floors of a building to deliver letters and other matter to be mailed into a letter box or other receptacle on the lower floor without the necessity of descending thereto."

The first patent issued to Cutler by the United States Patent Office specified that each mailbox must "be of metal, distinctly marked 'U.S. Letter Box'" with a slot labelled "letters," that "the door must open on hinges on one side, with the bottom not less than 2 ft. 6 in. above the floor," and that if installed in a building more than two stories high, the base of the mailbox must be padded with an elastic cushion to prevent damage to mail. The first Cutler-designed mailbox was installed in the Elwood Building in 1884, where it proved an instant success. It was displayed at expositions and word spread; installation in offices, railroads stations and public buildings soon followed suit in New York City and then beyond.

Standard mail chutes with openings for depositing mail. The illustration on the right demonstrates how the chute may be unlocked and opened to remove mail clogs. From Cutler brochure, 1937.

ART DECO MAILBOXES

The growing popularity of Cutler's device prompted Congress in 1893 to place mailbox and chute issues and concerns under the custody and regulation of the U.S. Post Office Department. And by permission of the Postal Service, 1905 saw mailboxes and chutes installed in hotels taller than five stories and apartment buildings with fifty residential units or more. As their locations grew more varied, mailbox designs became more sophisticated in both function and style. Although there were few permissible exceptions to Cutler's patented design directives, lobby receptacles evolved from simply utilitarian collection points to works of art.

A monopoly until 1904, Cutler's company manufactured approximately 1,600 systems for buildings across the United States; it would continue to do so for seventy years. Though no longer in production today, mailboxes remain a symbol of private–public partnership, commerce, and democracy. While some have been removed, forgotten, or painted over, others are polished daily, and hold pride of place in lobbies throughout the country. Their history is a true American story.

Cutler also offered twin mail chutes for taller buildings with higher volumes of mail.
From Cutler brochure, 1937.

INTRODUCTION

HISTORY AND DESIGN

"THE PATENT SYSTEM ADDED THE FUEL OF
INTEREST TO THE FIRE OF GENIUS."
— ABRAHAM LINCOLN, SIXTEENTH PRESIDENT
OF THE UNITED STATES, LAWYER,
AND HOLDER OF PATENT NO. 6469

On April 10, 1790, President George Washington signed into law the foundation of the United States' patent system. The Patent Act enabled inventors, for the first time in the country's history, to seek exclusive legal rights for their creations of "any useful art, manufacture, engine, machine, device, or any improvement thereon not before known or used." Applications, in the form of specifications, drawings, and models, were to be submitted to the newly established Patent Board, which had sole authority to grant patents for a period of fourteen years.

An early, ornate Cutler mailbox. From the University of Rochester's collection of original Cutler production line photographs.

After granting fifty-five patents, the first patent examiner, Thomas Jefferson, expanded the definition in 1793 to "any new and useful art, machine, manufacture or composition of matter and any new and useful improvement on any art, machine, and manufacture of composition of matter." The increased scope led to a dramatic uptick in applications, with ten thousand patents granted by 1836. That year, a new act brought the Patent Office under the purview of the State Department, which extended patent durations to a maximum of twenty-one years and implemented a new numbering system. Patents would no longer be identified by date and name, but by number. As such, Patent No. 1 was issued on July 13, 1836; all patents previously granted were relabeled with the suffix "X."

The nineteenth century saw the invention of electricity, steel, and petroleum, the locomotive, and the telephone; it was the age of scientific inquiry and technology, the second industrial revolution. Global competition drove innovation, and was the catalyst for America's first world's fair, the Exhibition of the Industry of All Nations, which opened on July 14, 1853. Held at New York City's Crystal Palace, on the site of what is now Bryant Park on Forty-second Street between Fifth and Sixth avenues, the New World's answer to London's Great Exhibition of 1851 showcased the latest and greatest innovations of the age. It attracted more than one million visitors over four months. Among its four-thousand-plus exhibits and displays of consumer goods, art works, and engineering advances were live demonstrations, among them a death-defying stunt by a young inventor from Vermont named Elisha Graves Otis.

Following a warm-up by showman P. T. Barnum, Otis introduced the world to the "safety elevator" by ascending an open elevator shaft in a suspended compartment and instructing his assistant to cut the cables to it with an axe. To the amazement of the assembled crowd, Otis did not plummet to his death, but remained hanging in mid-air—"All safe, gentlemen, all safe"—thanks to his spring-loaded governor to regulate the elevator's speed and a toothed safety brake. Otis's "Improvement in Hoisting Mechanism" held Patent No. 31,128.

CUTLER

MAIL CHUTES

SINCE 1883
THE STANDARD
OF EXCELLENCE

Mail Box No. 4740

CUTLER MAIL CHUTE CO.
ROCHESTER 7, N.Y.

Copyright 1956

The Cutler brochures from 1937 and 1956 present the Model 4740 mailbox from the Cutler standard line. One of these box models is still on view in the lobby of 730 Fort Washington Avenue and in several sites in the garment district of New York City.

By revolutionizing the centuries-old pulley-and-rope system, Otis's elevator made the rise of the modern skyline possible. It freed people from the need to climb many flights of stairs, and, aided by the development of steel building skeletons, the tall building—offices, commercial buildings, and residential buildings—began to rise in urban centers. The time was ripe for James Goold Cutler's invention.

"In the present age of multi-storied buildings, no builder or owner of such edifice has all the needful and convenient appliances," wrote the author of *The Industries of the City of Rochester: A Resume of Her Past, History and Progress in 1888*, "unless the Cutler U.S. Mail Chute is in use therein—a device as necessary for the business man as is the elevator."

Born in Albany, on April 24, 1848, James Goold Cutler moved to Rochester, New York, with his brother, J. W. Cutler, and their families in 1872. The city was a center of commerce, thanks to the building of the Erie Canal, which linked the Great Lakes with the Hudson River and New York City.

The new Model G Cutler chute, as advertised in the 1948 Cutler brochure, was embedded in the wall on three sides and had a transparent front panel through which the passage of deposited mail could be seen. It also included a "cigarette ejector" and was connected to many of the standard line boxes.

James Cutler became a practicing architect in Rochester, and found the platform for his achievements as an inventor, businessman, mayor, and patron. Cutler co-founded the short-lived firm Warner & Cutler (1875–77) with local architect Andrew Jackson Warner, but gained prominence in his own right as designer of such local landmarks as Kimball's Peerless Tobacco Factory (1880), a lavish mansion called "Kimball's Castle" (1882), and his own Cutler Building (1896). But it was the Elwood Building, Rochester's first "skyscraper," that would place his name in buildings all over the world.

From its location at the northeast corner of State and Main streets, the seven-story Elwood Building, built in 1879 for lawyer Frank Worcester Elwood, dominated "Four Corners," Rochester's busiest intersection. Cutler's design featured a Gothic clock tower that exaggerated the building's height, and was noted for its sixteen ornamental gargoyles, several of whom looked poised to attack the six-story Powers Building on the opposite corner. Commemorating the occupancy of the Elwood Building on October 25, 1879, the local newspaper *Union & Advertiser* hailed the block as a "credit to the city."

A photo of office staff using a mail chute, as featured in the 1948 Cutler catalog.

HISTORY AND DESIGN

At Elwood's suggestion, Cutler devised a metal chute that linked all the upper floors to the first-floor mailbox and allowed mail to be easily deposited from each floor. It was not the first device of its kind, but it proved superior to its predecessors, better ensuring that mail did not get trapped and damaged. The Post Office Department required that chutes be at least three-quarters-glass–fronted and accessible along their entire length to allow postal workers to locate and dislodge any trapped mail. James Cutler received thirty patents for modifications to his invention over the years, but few deviated far from the original plan.

The year after Cutler patented his design, he received a special award and a silver medal, respectively, at the New Orleans and Cincinnati expositions of 1884. That year, the first experimental mailbox and chute was installed in the Elwood Building, and other tests quickly followed in New York City office buildings, railroad stations, and public buildings. The Cutler Mail Chute Company was in business, through word-of-mouth and catalogs, which focused on the mailbox's indispensability as a time- and money-saver, and promised myriad benefits.

Before long, mailboxes and chutes were considered as essential to the operation of any major hotel, office, civic, or residential building as the front door. They took pride of place in the lobby and over time found a new role as decorative elements, available in a range of styles and materials.

Mailbox manufacturers and, soon, architects worked within the postal service's tight constraints to elevate the mere mail receptacle to a status symbol, an object whose design and workmanship could match those of its host building.

Satisfied customers and postal service officials alike lauded the usefulness of the Cutler mailbox and chute. In a letter to the author of *The Industries of the City of Rochester*, the assistant postmaster of Chicago, Collins S. Squires, wrote:

GENTLEMEN—IT GIVES US PLEASURE TO TESTIFY, AT YOUR REQUEST, TO THE PERFECT OPERATION OF THE U.S. MAIL CHUTE PLACED IN THE HOME INSURANCE BUILDING AND

THE RIALTO BUILDING, IN THIS CITY. THE VOLUME OF
MAIL IN THESE TWO BUILDINGS IS VERY GREAT, AND THE
CHUTES HAVE BEEN VERY SEVERELY TESTED. THE DEVICE
IS AN EXCELLENT ONE, OF GREAT VALUE TO THE POST-
OFFICE AS WELL AS TO THE PUBLIC, AND SHOULD COME
INTO GENERAL USE WITH AS LITTLE DELAY AS POSSIBLE.

———————————————————
———————————————

Though Cutler manufactured a number of different models, sizes, finishes, and designs, the company's trademark was the national bird of the
United States, the bald eagle. Some early mailboxes show it wearing a patri-
otic striped shield around its neck, while a Gothic iteration likely referenced
the gargoyle ornaments of its first home, the Elwood Building. Commonly
depicted with wings spread, clutching an olive branch in one claw and arrows
in the other, the Cutler eagles grew gradually more stylized over the years.
Later versions include a linear eagle that covered the entire surface of the
mailbox door. Then the eagle disappeared altogether in favor of more con-
temporary decorations.

The Cutler Mail Chute Company remained the sole manufacturer of the
mailbox and chute for two decades; during that time Cutler traveled exten-
sively and became an authority on civic problems, of which Rochester had no
shortage. After brief stints as president of the Rochester Chamber of Commerce from 1896, and Commissioner of Public Safety from 1900, he was
persuaded by ex-mayor of Rochester George Aldridge to run for the office
as a "Good Government" Republican. Inspired by the public works he had
seen in Europe, Cutler won a three-way election against James Johnson and
George E. Warren, and began the first of two successful two-year mayoral
terms on January 1, 1904.

Cutler's political life was not at the expense of his business, however; he
continued to oversee it throughout his mayoralty. In fact, the market for mail-

boxes and chutes had tightened considerably when the Capitol Mail Chute Company of Brooklyn, New York; the United States Mail Chute Corporation of Long Island City, New York; and the American Mailing Device Corporation of New York, New York (which claimed "clog-free" chutes) successfully applied for patents in 1904. Cutler changed tack in 1908, the year he left office, by cutting ties with Rochester firm Yawman & Erbe, which had manufactured the Cutler mailbox and chute since 1884, and establishing his own manufacturing operation. With his brother, Warren J. Cutler, installed as vice president and treasurer at a new, custom-built facility at 79-94 Anderson Street in Rochester, the renamed Cutler Manufacturing Company prepared to take on its rivals.

As mailbox manufacturers and locations grew more varied, the designs grew increasingly sophisticated in both function and style. Larger buildings accommodated outsized collection boxes, twin chutes, and separate systems for letters and packages. And the designs proliferated, taking on the dominant styles of the times.

The classic Cutler mailbox bore the company name in no less than three places—on a tag that hung from the eagle's neck, on a banner beneath the eagle, and in bold print across the bottom. Cutler's competitors developed their own identifying design elements—Capitol Mail Chute's Capitol dome, and American Mailing Device Corporation's caduceus, the serpent-entwined staff of Mercury.

Common to all was the symbolism of grand ideas—patriotism, democracy, integrity. Mailing a letter was serious business, a transaction that transformed private into federal property, bound by federal law, at the instant

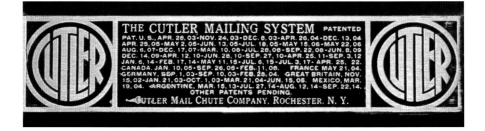

Many Cutler installations had a band on the chute, just above the box, that listed all current patents from the date of manufacture and protected various design features.

of mailing. Hence, mailbox imagery and advertising was reverent and easily recognizable by the public, whose trust was essential. Cutler's 1917 catalog featured an illustration of a stamp transporting a letter around the world with ease, while a letter remained stranded on the upper floors of a chuteless building. Most advertisements emphasized the official nature of the mailbox chute by noting that every installation required Postal Service approval.

While the eagle symbolized patriotism and strength, another figure graced some mailboxes: Mercury spoke to the magical element of transporting a letter to the other side of the world—or from the one-hundredth to the first floor—through the simple of act of dropping it through a slot. The messenger of the gods and the god of commerce and travel in Roman mythology, Mercury first adorned the seal of the U.S. Postal Service in 1872, under then-Postmaster General Ebenezer Hazard, long before the eagle graced Cutler's mailboxes, and became a common figure on mailboxes, presented in full figure, often in flight, or symbolized by his helmet or a staff entwined with serpents holding an envelope.

Behind the scenes, the mailbox business was changing. On May 9, 1909, the *New York Times* reported that the Cutler Manufacturing Company, the Automatic Mail Delivery Company, and the Coburn-Gahren Construction Company had merged to form a new $2,000,000 corporation ("Mail Chute Men in Merger"). The deal was the conclusion, in Cutler's favor, of patent disputes between the two mailbox entities, and, according to the *Times*, it united, "practically all the mail chute companies in the market." From its new offices in New York City's Times building, the once-again-rebranded

The gothic Cutler eagle, as displayed on the front of the original factory building in Rochester. This eagle emblem appeared on most Cutler mailboxes until the 1930s.

Cutler Mail Chute Company took over the property, contracts, and businesses of both companies. James Cutler was named president; Automatic's Frank E. Anderson became vice president.

The merger stoked the discontent of Cutler's remaining business rivals, who called for greater scrutiny of his business practices and what they perceived as his suspiciously close relationship with the Post Office Department. Congressional hearings in 1911 on the department's expenditures contained testimony from Edwin Fairfax Naulty, president and general manager of the Fairfax United Mail Chute System, which asserted that the Post Office had fostered a monopoly on placement of Cutler's products within government buildings and issued excessive bonded contracts that limited competition. The clear implication was that the Post Office Department favored the Cutler Mail Chute Company, and in doing so allowed the company to engage in price fixing.

Despite Cutler's denials of collusion or wrongdoing, the federal government decided shortly after the hearings to recognize the rights of Capitol Mail Chute, the United States Mail Chute Corporation, and the American Mailing Device Corporation to service U.S. mail, and added to the list the Federal Mail Chute Corp. of San Francisco, California (which later merged with Cutler); the Pioneer Mail Chute Corporation of Carlstadt, New Jersey; and the Lewis Sack Company of Somerville, Massachusetts (which manufactured only collection boxes).

Cutler retired from business shortly afterward, in 1915, but continued to serve his beloved Rochester, a civic figure and patron until his death in 1927. Along with ex-mayor George W. Aldridge, Cutler was appointed to the city's newly created Municipal Art Commission, whose remit was to approve public art acquisitions or alterations. In 1922 he donated $10,000 to the University of Rochester to endow a series of lectures, and was honored in return with the naming of the Gordon and Kaelber–designed Cutler Union on University Avenue. Once a part of the women's campus, the building now houses administrative offices for the Memorial Art Gallery.

The evolution of mailbox design reflected the sweeping trends of late-nineteenth and early twentieth-century architecture, and the firms that led them. A number of notable architecture firms collaborated with Cutler and other manufacturers to produce unique or special-line designs. On occasion, they elected to design every last detail of their building lobbies, down to the mailboxes, as integral elements of the architecture. There were few creative constraints in mailbox design, and the sea change from classical to Art Deco was a microcosm of the new aesthetics and ideas taking hold in architecture at large.

Among the earliest Cutler collaborators was Chicago architect and urban planner Daniel H. Burnham (1846–1912). Together with John Wellborn Root, Burnham was renowned for the design and construction of the World's Columbian Exposition, which came to fruition two years after Root's death, in 1893. As a solo architect, one of Burnham's most famous commissions was the Flatiron Building (1902) at 175 Fifth Avenue, New York City. Named for its wedge-like shape, the Flatiron Building was conceived as a classical Greek column with Beaux-Arts styling. Early sketches of its limestone and glazed terra-cotta façade were rather more elaborate than the built result, and showed a clock face that was never executed and an elaborate crown. Burnham collaborated with Cutler on its mailbox.

The Flatiron Building was one of the tallest buildings in the city, and one of only two skyscrapers north of Fourteenth Street. That designation

ART DECO MAILBOXES

was changed, however, in 1913 with the construction of Cass Gilbert's Woolworth Building (1913) at 233 Broadway. Zanesville, Ohio–born Gilbert (1859–1934) was a skyscraper pioneer, who took the innovation of Chicago skyscraper architects a step further, and higher, by using a steel frame. He designed the Woolworth Building in the neo-Gothic style, in keeping with his belief that public buildings should reflect tradition and humanist values such as democracy, law, and order. At sixty stories and 792 feet, the Woolworth Building was the tallest skyscraper in the world upon completion. Its neo-Gothic lobby is decorated in veined marble and contains a vaulted ceiling, mosaics, a stained-glass skylight, bronze furnishings—and four Gilbert-designed brass and marble mailboxes

The Woolworth Building was surpassed in height, twice, in 1930, following a race between the Bank of Manhattan Trust and Chrysler buildings to become the tallest in the world. At 927 feet, the former held the title for one week, until the Chrysler Building's spire, which was constructed in secret from inside the building, took its full height to 1,045 feet. It remains the tallest brick building in the world today. Brooklyn architect William Van Alen (1883-1954) designed the skyscraper, located at 405 Lexington Avenue, for William P. Chrysler, founder of the Chrysler automotive company. Its exterior gargoyles depict Chrysler car ornaments and its spire is reminiscent of a radiator grille. While its exterior drew mixed reviews from critics at the time, its Art Deco lobby, with marble floors and two architect-designed mailboxes, was an instant hit.

The Chrysler's brief supremacy ended in 1931 with the completion of the 1,454-foot Empire State Building. Located at 350 Fifth Avenue, the Art Deco icon and its complementary mailboxes were designed by the newly formed firm Shreve, Lamb & Harmon. R. H. Shreve of Canada and William Lamb of Brooklyn had met at the firm Carrère & Hastings and formed Shreve & Lamb in 1924; they were joined by Chicago architect Arthur Loomis Harmon in 1929, when construction on the Empire State Building was already underway, and remained in business until the mid-1970s.

The New York City-based firm Cross & Cross frequently collaborated with Cutler but also produced its own mailbox designs. A partnership of brothers John Walter Cross (1878–1951) and Eliot Cross (1884–1949), it

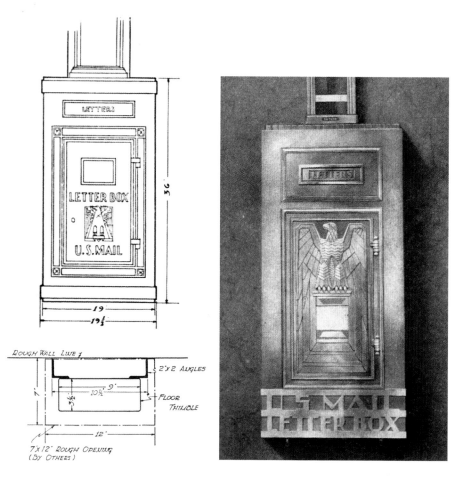

was renowned for its Art Deco skyscrapers and upscale residential commissions. Among Cross & Cross's most significant works are the General Electric Building (1931) – known as the RCA Building until 1988 – at 570 Lexington Avenue and the landmarked office building 90 Broad Street (1932). The latter's Beaux-Arts lobby contains a barrel-vaulted ceiling, gold-leaf detailing, and an architect-designed mailbox by the elevator.

James Cutler did not live to see the construction of the Empire State or Chrysler buildings, or the explosion of Art Deco from coast to coast, in fashion, furnishings, architecture, and the decorative arts. But the new direction of "mail-chute boxes" was the subject of a June 1931 portfolio in the journal *Architecture*— "56th in a series of collections of photographs illustrating various minor architectural details." The featured mailboxes demonstrated the creative range on display across the lobbies of America and the newfound architectural importance of the device.

Amid the building boom of the 1930s, the Cutler company also released its first "Model G" mail chutes. Stronger, extra-reinforced, and partially recessed, these were a response to rising smoking rates, and the associated risks to buildings and mail: a cigarette-ejecting mechanism was built into each access pocket.

As Art Deco gave way to the minimalism of Modernism, mailboxes became noticeably more restrained. The company's later catalogs targeted the market for building renovation and remodeling by focusing on the durability and flexibility of its products and advertised streamlined versions of its signature models. Now a manufacturing veteran, the company boasted of the wide range of buildings that owned or leased its mailboxes and the endless

These mailbox designs from the Cutler line, shown in the company's 1937 brochure, can still be seen in many buildings. Model 4083 (above, left) featured Cutler's first art deco eagle, a variation of which is still on display at 565 West End Avenue in New York City. Model 4770 (above, center) features another, slightly later art deco eagle design, examples of which can still be seen in The Milford New York Hotel and a number of other midtown hotels. Model 4165 (above, right) was Cutler's standard mailbox design, in place in hundreds of buildings.

HISTORY AND DESIGN

variety of available slot sizes, padlock styles, finishes, fittings, and specifications.

In 1974 the Cutler Manufacturing Company left New York for Lakeland, Florida, where it expired, decades after its competitors had gone out of business. While few new chutes were built after 1980, many remained in place and active in the late 1990s, including 360 in Chicago, more than 900 in Manhattan and the Bronx, and hundreds more around the world. Among them can be seen three located in the Waldorf-Astoria Hotel, three at Grand Central Terminal, and four in the Empire State Building in New York City; seven in Philadelphia's City Hall. The rarest is arguably a circa-1900 Cutler model in the historic Lenox Hotel in Boston's Back Bay, one of the few Cutler mailchutes still functioning. Others, such as those in New York's Chrysler and RCA buildings, and Chicago's hundred-story John Hancock Center, remain visible but were sealed after repeated jams.

In 1997, the National Fire Protection Association (NFPA) banned the use of mail chutes in all new building construction, ensuring the demise of an industry that was already deep in decline. Citing concerns that vertical shafts, like chimneys, could spread smoke to all floors in the event of a fire, the NFPA introduced a new code at a time when

The 1939 Cutler brochure advertised a variety of art deco box designs, some standard, some special.

mail chutes were gradually being replaced by modern mailrooms.

Not only are mailrooms safer, but they also handle incoming mail and eliminate the problem of mail-chute jams. Cutler's improvements notwithstanding, oversized or improperly folded mail regularly jammed chutes, resulting in damage and significant delays. In a famous instance, forty thousand pieces of mail became stuck between the lobby and the basement at New York City's McGraw-Hill building at 330 West 42nd Street. Extricating them required removing cinder blocks between the floors, and the use of twenty-three mail sacks to catch the resulting avalanche. The lobby mailbox and the chutes are gone.

Nevertheless, Cutler's presence is still visible today—in the eagle medallion on the exterior of 74-76 Anderson Avenue (now Rochester Lead Works Company), in the souvenir plates, doors, mail-chute segments, and padlocks that regularly come up at auction, and, above all, in the mailboxes that remain in place across the country and around the world. Whether wall mounted, inset to mimic a picture frame on a wall, or concealed in alcoves, stairwells, or service closets, James Cutler's invention outlasted its function to become a thing of beauty.

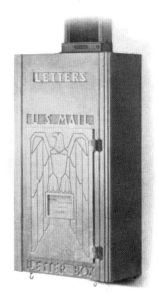

The astonishing mailbox in the lobby of 570 Lexington Avenue, New York City.

GALLERY
OF
MAILBOXES

1890s

St. James Building, 1129-1137 Broadway, New York, NY,
Cutler (Bruce Price, 1898).

1900s

The Lenox Hotel, 710 Boylston Street, Boston, MA, Cutler (1900).

The Textile Building, 66 Leonard Street, New York, NY, Henry J. Hardenbergh (1901, though this mailbox was likely installed at a later date).

ART DECO MAILBOXES

The Flatiron Building, 175 Fifth Avenue, New York, NY,
Cutler with Daniel Burnham (1902).
Upon completion, the Flatiron Building was the tallest building in the city. It was originally named
the Fuller Building after George A. Fuller, founder of the Fuller Company and "father of the
skyscraper," but quickly came to be known by its wedge-like shape.

The St. Regis Hotel, 2-12 East 55th Street, New York, NY,
Cutler with Sloan & Robertson (1904).

ART DECO MAILBOXES

Liberty Tower, 55 Liberty Street, New York, NY,
Cutler with Henry Ives Cobb (1910).

GALLERY OF MAILBOXES

Trinity Buildings, 111-113 Broadway, New York, NY, Cutler (Francis H. Kimball, 1905).

GALLERY OF MAILBOXES

ART DECO MAILBOXES

Alwyn Court, 180 West 58th Street, New York, NY, Cutler (Harde & Short, 1909).
This is a unique Cutler box with a hammered finish, an unusual eagle, and a specially-designed plate opening for a mail chute.

ART DECO MAILBOXES

The Rockfall, 545 West 111th Street, New York, NY, Cutler (1909). Featured in the
University of Rochester's original collection of Cutler production photographs.

1910s

The Woolworth Building, 233 Broadway, New York, NY, Cass Gilbert (1913).
One of the oldest skyscrapers in the U.S., the Woolworth Building was also the tallest –
at 60 stories – from 1930 to 1931. It's Neo-Gothic- style lobby is decorated in Skyros
veined marble and contains a vaulted ceiling, mosaics, a stained-glass skylight, bronze
furnishings, and four Gilbert-designed mailboxes.

331 Madison Avenue. Charles Berg, Severence & Van Alen. (1911)

Grand Central Terminal, 87 East 42nd Street, New York, NY, Cutler (Reed & Stem / Warren & Wetmore, 1913). Grand Central Terminal was constructed between 1903 and 1913 to replace the previous station on the site, Grand Central Station, hence the common confusion with its name. The station itself was designed by Reed & Stem, but Warren & Wetmore was responsible for its Beaux-Arts style and interior architectural details, which include four Cutler mailboxes, set on the upper and lower concourses.

1920s

Hotel Pennsylvania, 401 Seventh Avenue, New York, NY, American Mailing Device
(McKim, Mead & White, 1920).
Features the hotel's initials enclosed by a wreath.

Above: The Common Ground's Times Square Hotel, 255 West 43rd Street, New York, NY,
Cutler (Gronenberg & Leuchtag, 1924).

Opposite: 183 Madison Avenue, New York, NY,
American Mailing Device (Warren & Wetmore, 1924).

ART DECO MAILBOXES

Standard Oil Building, 26 Broadway, New York, NY,
Cutler (Carrere & Hastings / Shreve, Lamb & Blake / Kimball & Thompson, 1924).

ART DECO MAILBOXES

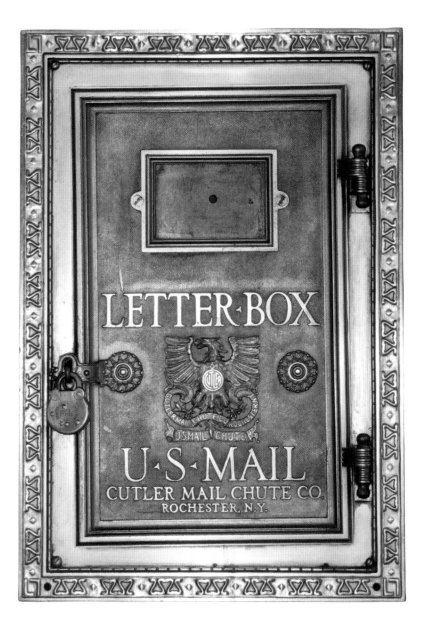

LeVeque Tower, 50 West Broad Street, Columbus, OH,
Cutler (Charles Howard Crane/Thomas W. Lamb, 1924).
At 555-ft. 6-in., LeVeque Tower remained Columbus' tallest building until 1974,
when it was surpassed by the Rhodes State Office Tower. The lobby features a bronze
plaque with the horoscope of the tower and the position of the planets at the time of the
laying of the cornerstone (February 12, 1925) set into the floor.

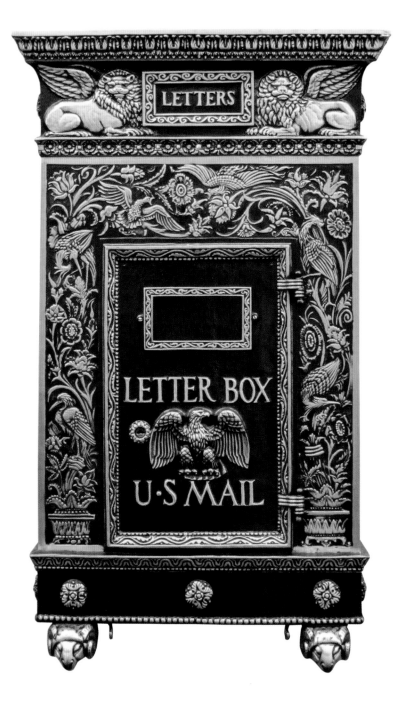

550 7th Avenue, New York, NY, Buchman & Kahn (1925)

60 Centre Street, Court House, New York, Guy Lowell (1926)

GALLERY OF MAILBOXES

LETTER·BOX

U·S·MAIL

CUTLER MAIL CHUTE CO.
ROCHESTER N.Y.

200 Madison Avenue,
Warren & Wetmore. Two different styles of Cutler mailboxes (1926)

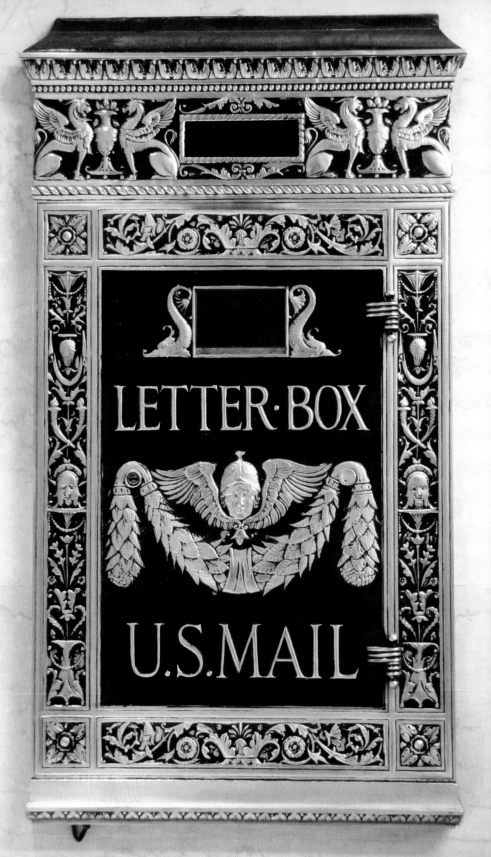

LETTER·BOX

U.S.MAIL

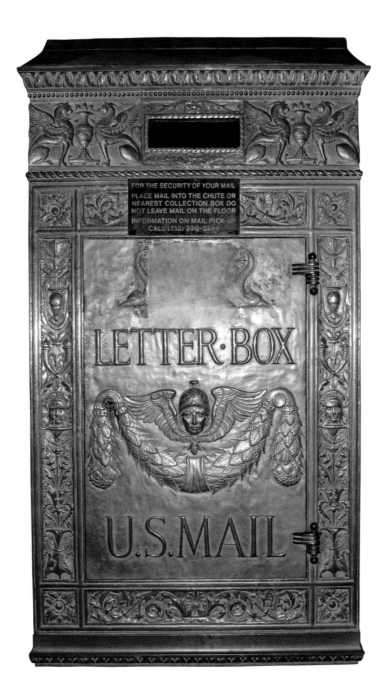

The Transportation Building, 225 Broadway, New York, NY, York & Sawyer (1927).
This mailbox's appearance changed dramatically with a detailed painting.

The Paramount Building, 1501 Broadway, New York, NY, Rapp and Rapp (1927). The lobby of the landmarked Paramount Building was modeled after the Paris Opera House, with white marble columns, balustrades, and a grand staircase.

ART DECO MAILBOXES

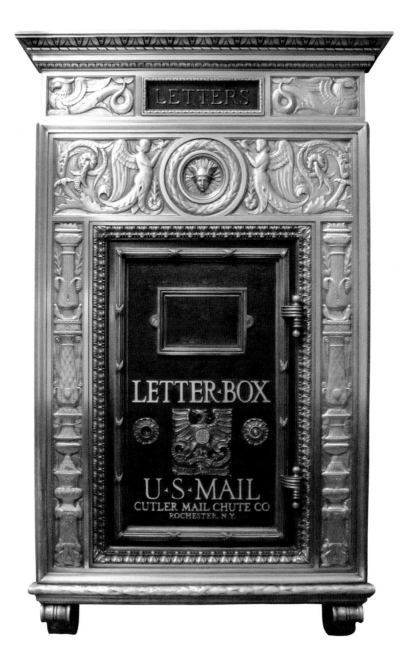

Above: The Sherry-Netherland, 781 Fifth Avenue, New York, NY,
Cutler with Schultze & Weaver/ Buchman & Kahn (1927).

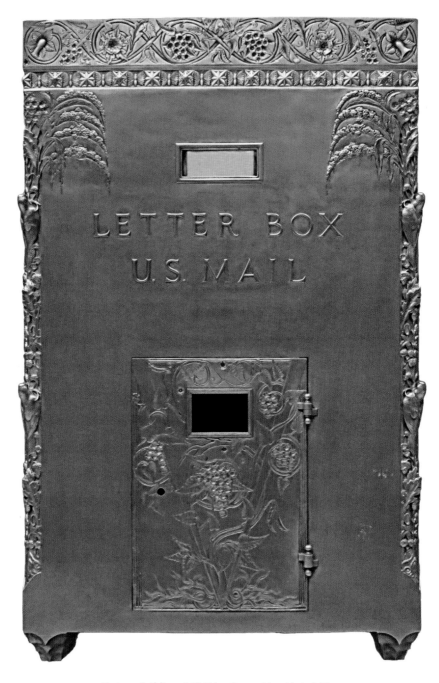

Verizon Building, 140 West Street, New York, NY,
Ralph Walker with McKenzie, Voorhees & Gmelin (1927).

ART DECO MAILBOXES

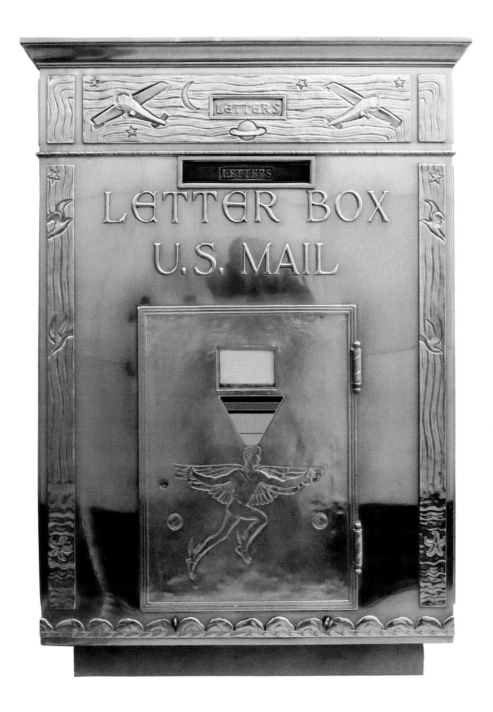

205 East 42nd Street, New York, NY, Starrett & Van Vleck (1927).

GALLERY OF MAILBOXES

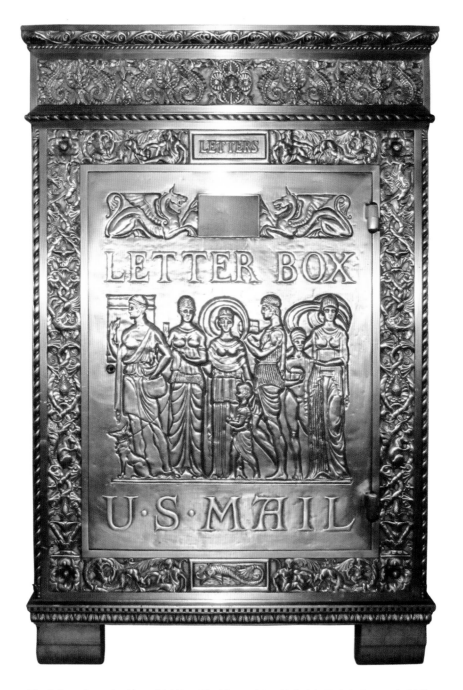

The Salmon Tower building, 11 West 42nd Street, New York, NY, York & Sawyer (1927). The figures on the doorway of this building are echoed on the mailbox.

THIS IS A
NO SMOKING
AREA

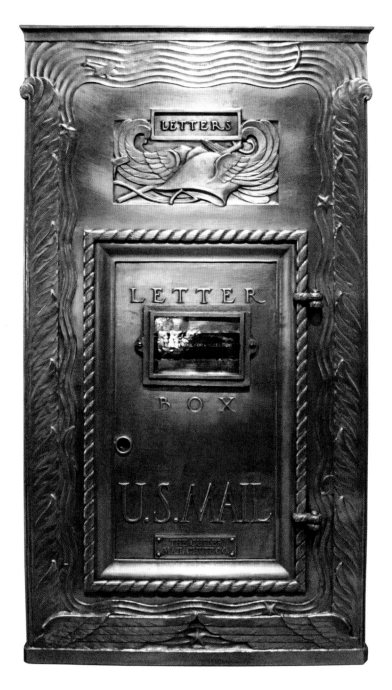

1 Fifth Avenue, New York, NY,
Cutler with Helme, Corbett & Harrison / Sugarman & Berger (1927).

ART DECO MAILBOXES

The Navarre Building, 512 7th Avenue, New York, NY, Sugarman & Berger (1928).

GALLERY OF MAILBOXES

Above: 2 Park Avenue, New York, NY, Buchman & Kahn (1928).

Opposite: The Film Center Building, 630 Ninth Avenue, New York, NY,
Buchman & Kahn (1928).
The Film Center Building's Art Deco-style first-floor interior was designated a New York
City landmark in 1982, and is dominated by stylized movie imagery, such as cylinders
recalling film cannisters, cameras, and other three-dimensional motifs.

Above: The Milford, 700 8th Avenue, New York, NY,
Cutler (Schwartz & Gross, 1928). Cutler Art Deco eagle.

Opposite: The International Telephone and Telegraph Building,
75 Broad Street, New York, NY, Buchman & Kahn (1928).

ART DECO MAILBOXES

48 Wall Street, New York, NY, Benjamin Wistar Morris (1928).

ART DECO MAILBOXES

51 Madison Avenue, NY Life Building, Cass Gilbert (1928). Motifs on the sides of the box portray various ways of transporting mail.

GALLERY OF MAILBOXES

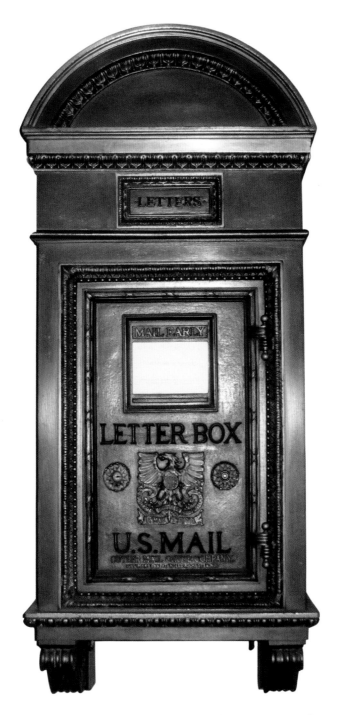

The Apthorp, 2211 Broadway, New York, NY, Cutler (Clinton & Russell, 1928). Exterior mailbox, located under archway.

ART DECO MAILBOXES

Walker Tower, 212 West 18th Street, New York, NY, Ralph Walker (1929).

GALLERY OF MAILBOXES

Above: 500 Fifth Avenue, New York, NY, Cutler with Shreve, Lamb & Harmon (1929).
Shreve, Lamb & Harmon designed the Art Deco office tower, 500 Fifth Avenue, in the
year construction began on the Empire State Building. Its mailbox's enlongated eagles
echo those on the building exterior.

Opposite: 336 Central Park West, Schwartz & Gross (1928).

GALLERY OF MAILBOXES

Above: 575 7th Avenue/1441 Broadway, New York, NY, Buchman & Kahn (1929).

Opposite: The Fuller Building, 595 Madison Avenue, New York, NY,
Walker & Gillette (1929).
The lobby of the landmarked Fuller Building features marble walls,
mosaic floors and bronze details.

ART DECO MAILBOXES

One Hanson Place, Brooklyn, NY, Halsley, McCormack & Helmer (1929).
One Hanson Place is located in Brooklyn's Fort Greene neighborhood and was once
the borough's tallest building – at 28, 512 ft. Designed in the Spanish Revival style by
Halsley, McCormack & Helmer, it is now a landmarked residential building. Its painted-
black mailbox features Eqyptian and astrological motifs.

The New Yorker Hotel, 481 8th Avenue, New York, NY, Cutler (1929).
Large Cutler mailbox set into the floor rather than the wall.

GALLERY OF MAILBOXES

75 Federal Street, Boston, MA, Cutler with Thomas M. James (1929).

ART DECO MAILBOXES

540 Broad Street, Newark, NJ, Voorhees, Gmelin & Walker (1929).
Large, floor-standing box decorated with vines and flowers.

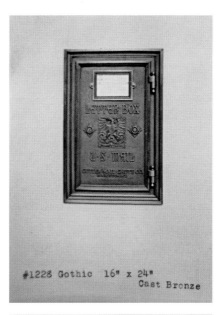

#1228 Gothic 16" x 24"
Cast Bronze

#3382-A 29½" x 16" Cast Bronze

The Willoughby Tower, 8 South Michigan Avenue, Chicago, IL,
Cutler (Samuel Crowen & Associates, 1929).
The Willoughby Tower stands 280 ft. tall on the site of the former 8-story
Willoughby Building. Its lobby is trimmed in solid cast- and green Italian bronze
and features a Gothic-style Cutler.

— 89 —

THIS MAIL BOX IS
AN HISTORIC RESTORATION
AND NOT IN USE.

MAIL BOXES ARE LOCATED
TO YOUR RIGHT.

Above: 1608 Walnut Street, Philadelphia, PA, Tilden, Register & Pepper (1929).

Opposite: Penn Center Suburban Station, 16th Street and JFK Boulevard, Philadelphia, PA, Graham, Anderson, Probst & White (1929).

ART DECO MAILBOXES

Carbide & Carbon Building, 230 North Michigan Avenue, Chicago, IL,
Burnham & Burnham (1929).
Now the Chicago Hard Rock Hotel, the Carbide & Carbon Building was designed
to resemble a green champagne bottle. Its architect-designed mailbox resides in the
building's original lobby on Michigan Avenue.

ART DECO MAILBOXES

230 Congress Street, Boston, MA

1930s

1 North LaSalle Street, Chicago, IL, Vitzhum & Burns (1930).

Above: 99 Hudson Street, New York, NY, U.S. Mail Chute (Victor Mayper, 1930).
U.S. Mail Chute model discovered in the basement storage room.

Opposite: The London Terrace Apartments, 401-411 West 23rd Street, New York, NY,
Cutler (Farrar & Watmough, 1930).
While the London Terrace Apartments at 401-411 West 23rd Street were built in 1930,
the building's Cutler mailboxes display both the company's Rochester and Florida
address – which suggests that some were installed later. The Renaissance Revival-style
complex comprises 14 contiguous buildings over an entire city block, making it one of
the largest apartment buildings in the world.

Above: 435 West 50th Street, New York, NY, Voorhees, Gmelin & Walker
The design of this box mirrors the geometry of the building front.

Opposite: Circle Tower, 55 Monument Circle, Indianapolis, IN, Rubush & Hunter (1930).
Circle Tower forms part of Indianapolis' Washington Street-Monument Circle Historic
District and is listed on the National Register of Historic Places. Its three-part mailbox is
set between the elevators and depicts an underwater fantasy theme.

ART DECO MAILBOXES

Above: Kings County Hospital, T-Building, 451 Clarkson Avenue, Brooklyn, NY (1930).

Opposite: Times Square Building, 45 Exchange Boulevard, Rochester, NY,
Voorhees, Gmelin & Walker (1930).
The Times Square Building dominates the Rochester skyline with
four 42-ft.-high aluminum wings that weigh 12,000 pounds each.

ART DECO MAILBOXES

Above: 116 John Street/1 Platt Street, New York, NY,
Cutler with Louis A. Abramson (1930).

Opposite: The Chrysler Building, 393-413 Lexington Avenue, New York, NY,
William Van Alen / Reinhard, Hofmeister & Walquist (1930).
The Chrysler Building was the tallest building in the world until 1931, when the Empire
State Building surpassed it, but it remains the tallest brick building in the world today.
Its marble-, onyx- and amber-clad lobby contains two architect-designed mailboxes.

GALLERY OF MAILBOXES

Above: 1616 Walnut Street, Philadelphia, PA, Tilden, Register & Pepper (1930).
Upon completion of 1616 Walnut Street, Tilden, Register & Pepper won an award for
their design at the 12th International Buildings Congress in Budapest, Hungary.

Opposite: Former Western Union Building, 60 Hudson Street, New York, NY,
Voorhees, Gmelin & Walker (1930).
The former Western Union Building's interior and German Expressionism-influenced
exterior were designated New York City Landmarks in 1991.

GALLERY OF MAILBOXES

80 Eighth Avenue, New York, NY, William Whitehall (1930).

ART DECO MAILBOXES

120 Wall Street, New York, NY, Buchman & Kahn (1930).

GALLERY OF MAILBOXES

The Empire State Building, 350 Fifth Avenue, New York, NY,
Shreve, Lamb & Harmon (1931).
An icon of Art Deco, the 102-story Empire State Building stands 1,454-ft. tall
at the corner of Fifth Avenue and West 34th Street. Its world-famous lobby is
one of few interiors to be designated a historic landmark by the Landmarks
Preservation Committee and features grand murals, chandeliers, extensive
gold leaf and its vertical-striped mailboxes.

ART DECO MAILBOXES

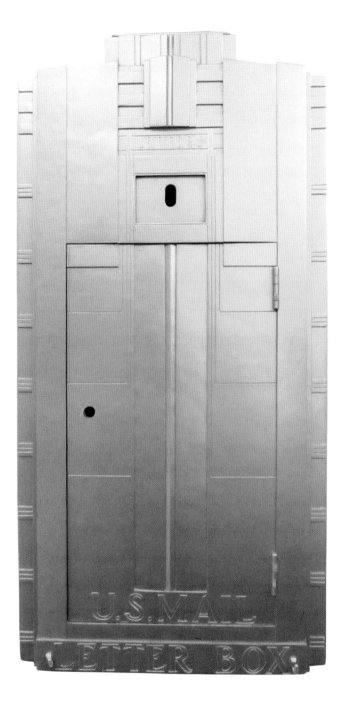

Belltel Lofts, 365 Brooklyn Bridge Street, Brooklyn, NY.
Voorhees, Gmelin & Walker (1930).

GALLERY OF MAILBOXES

Above: 29 Broadway, New York, NY, Sloan & Robertson (1931).
In a reversal of Post Office specifications, this mailbox door has hinges on the left
and the lock on the right, incorporated into the design as the headlight on the
front of a locomotive. This box features then-contemporary symbols of progress, modes
of travel, and movement of the mail.

Opposite: 80 Broad Street, New York, NY, Sloan & Robertson (1931).
With its lettering position and shape, this architect-designed mailbox challenged
Post Office-imposed design restrictions.

The Brill Building, 1619 Broadway, New York, NY, Victor Bark Jr. (1931).
Also known as the Alan E. Lefcourt Building, the Brill Building is famed for housing
music industry offices and studios.

ART DECO MAILBOXES

20 Exchange Place, New York, NY, Cross & Cross (1931).
Southwestern-inspired design featuring flowers and a rising sun.

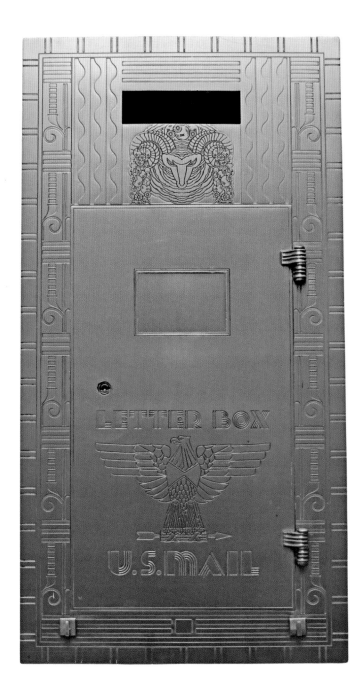

The Ardsley Apartments, 320 Central Park West, New York, NY, Emery Roth (1931).
Etched-line ram's head design with horns as cornucopias.

The Waldorf-Astoria Hotel, 301 Park Avenue, New York, NY,
Schultze & Weaver (1931).
The Waldorf-Astoria Hotel is famed for its block-through lobby, which is paneled in dark
Oregon maple. The hotel features four architect-designed mailboxes.

General Electric Building, 570 Lexington Avenue, New York, NY,
Cross & Cross (1931).
The landmarked General Electric Building is decorated with diagonal and zigzag motifs
on the exterior to evoke electricity. Its integrated, architect-designed floor-to-ceiling
mailbox is the centerpiece of the lobby.

GALLERY OF MAILBOXES

1 Wall Street, New York, NY,
Cutler with Ralph Walker of Voorhees, Gmelin & Walker (1931).
The atypical design for 1 Wall Street (1931), originally the Irving Trust Company
Building, incorporates a zig zag limestone "curtain wall" on the exterior,
echoed in this mailbox.

ART DECO MAILBOXES

The Johns-Manville Building, 273-277 Madison Avenue, New York, NY,
Kenneth Franzheim (1931).

GALLERY OF MAILBOXES

The DuMont Building, 515 Madison Avenue, New York, NY,
Cutler (J.E.R. Carpenter, 1931).

ART DECO MAILBOXES

The Newsweek Building, 432-450 Madison Avenue, New York, NY,
Kohn, Vitolo & Knight (1931).

GALLERY OF MAILBOXES

Above: Stonehenge 113, 501 West 113th Street, New York, NY,
Capitol Mail Chute Co. (George F. Pelham, 1931).

Opposite: Bank of America Building (1931), 20 South Broadway, Yonkers, NY,
U.S. Mail Chute with William P. Katz (1931).

ART DECO MAILBOXES

Above: Carew Tower, 1 West Fifth Street, Cincinnati, OH,
Cutler with Richard Rauh & Associates (1931).

Opposite: First Merit Tower, 106 Main Street, Akron, OH, Walter & Weeks (1931).
Also known as the First National Bank Building, First Merit Tower remains
the tallest building in Akron.

GALLERY OF MAILBOXES

Netherland Plaza Hotel, 35 West Fifth Street, Cincinnati, OH,
Cutler with Richard Rauh & Associates (1931).

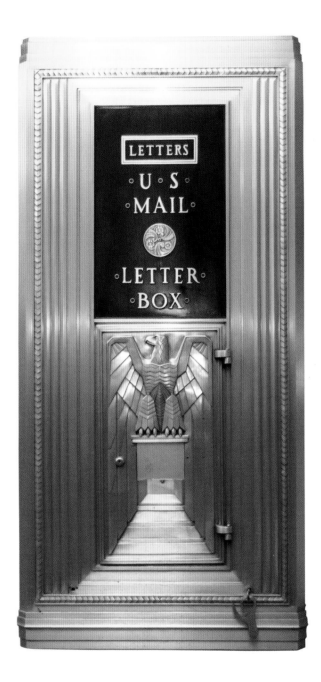

Above: 744 Broad Street, Newark, NJ. John J. & Wilson C. Eli, Cutler (1931).

Opposite: The Rivage, 21 West Street, New York, NY. Starrett & van Vleck (1931).

ART DECO MAILBOXES

Above: 90 Broad Street, New York, NY, Cross & Cross (1932).
Cross & Cross' landmarked prewar office building contains a dramatic Beaux Arts
lobby. Its barrel-vaulted ceiling and gold-leaf detailing are complemented by the
architect-designed mailbox by the elevator.

Opposite: The Continental Bank & Trust Company Building,
30 Broad Street, New York, NY, Cutler with Morris & O'Connor (1932).

GALLERY OF MAILBOXES

Above: Philadelphia National Bank Building,
1 South Broad Street, Philadelphia, PA, John Torrey Windrim (1932).
The Philadelphia National Bank Building is the tallest building in the
city east of Broad Street. It is home to the world's largest ringing bell, the
"Founder's Bell," which can be heard for 25 miles around.

Opposite: Wagner Building, 2488 Grand Concourse, Bronx, NY,
U.S. Mail Chute (1931).

Above: 1528 Walnut Street, Philadelphia, PA, Paul Phillipe Cret (1932).

Opposite: The American International Building, 66-76 Pine Street, New York, NY, Cutler with Clinton & Russell / Holton & George (1932).

GALLERY OF MAILBOXES

Above: 2 Wall Street, New York, NY (Walker & Gillette, 1933).

Opposite: The Thomas J. Moyer Ohio Judicial Center,
65 South Front Street, Columbus, OH, Harry Hake (1933).
The landmarked Thomas J. Moyer Ohio Judicial Center was designed by Cincinnati
architect Harry Hake and originally known as the Ohio Departments Building.

— 136 —

ART DECO MAILBOXES

Above: 30th Street Station, 2955 Market Street, Philadelphia, PA,
Cutler with Graham, Anderson, Probst & White (1933).

Opposite: The LaSalle Bank Building, 135 South LaSalle Street, Chicago, IL,
Graham, Anderson, Probst & White (1934).
Now the Bank of America Building, the LaSalle Bank Building was built during the
Great Depression and remained the last skyscraper to be built in Chicago until One
Prudential in 1955. The mailbox is a model of the building itself, with the windows
containing lights to show the location of the elevators.

ART DECO MAILBOXES

Above: Knickerbocker Village, Monroe Street, New York, NY,
Frederick Ackerman (1934).

Opposite: The Thurgood Marshall United States Courthouse, 40 Centre Street,
New York, NY, Capitol Mail Chute (Cass Gilbert and Cass Gilbert Jr., 1936).
The Thurgood Marshall United States Courthouse's soaring marble lobby features two
Capitol Mail Chute models.

Above: 275 Seventh Avenue, New York, NY, Cutler with Buchman & Kahn (1936).

ART DECO MAILBOXES

411 West End Avenue, New York, NY, Capitol Mail Chute (George F. Pelham Jr., 1936).

GALLERY OF MAILBOXES

565 West End Avenue, Cutler with Hyman Isaac Feldman (1937).

ART DECO MAILBOXES

Castle Village Complex, 120-200 Cabrini Boulevard, New York, NY, George F. Pelham, Jr., Capitol Mail Chute (1938).

730 Fort Washington Avenue, New York, NY, J. M. Felson.
Art deco Cutler mailbox with no eagle (1939).

CREDITS

All photographs by the author unless otherwise indicated.

The author wishes to acknowledge the following for permission to take and include photographs and illustrations:

INDEX

[Buildings referred to or pictured in text are listed under the city in which they are located and by building name. Page numbers in *italic* refer to captions.]